I0673652

Unearthed

Unearthed

poems and prose by
Sherwanda Y. Chism, Ed.D.

Printed in the United States of America

First Printing, 2022

ISBN 979-8-218-00785-0

Cover & Interior Design by Visions Promotional Agency
www.vpromoagency.com

For writers who have allowed the husher's voice to become louder than theirs. You are a treasure. Tell your stories.

Forward-

By Trinity Chism

Mama's words will cradle you, bring you joy, convict you, sing you to sleep, minister to you, reassure you, protect you, bring you peace, and redeem you.

When you are wrong, these words will sting but gift wrap you in love. These words will wipe away your tears.

My Mama's words will do what others' words cannot. They will run through your veins and trickle down to your feet so that you can walk in your truth.

Mama's words.

Unearthed

Unearth- to dig up; to discover; to bring to light [1]

I let hurt blind me
Caused me to fall so deep
Buried by bitter poisoning

Unearthed:
Debriding, so I can come clean
Shedding dead things that were attached to me
Snatching back the layers that smothered me
Tilling through the rocky pieces of me
Shovels and wheelbarrows collecting
Samples of what I used to be
Get this shhhhh off me
Must tell it so I can heal me

Unearthed-
Who said I can't be happy
That peace I don't deserve
Who said I have to get used to the inflammation of hurt

Unearthed:
Delivered and set free
No longer bound by uncertainty
Was blind but now I see
The light and smell of sweet victory

1 "Unearth." *Merriam-Webster.com*, 2022. https://www.merriam-webster.com/dictionary/unearth (4 June 2022)

Unearthed:
I don't have to feel shame

Unearthed:
I'm clearing my name

Contents

Crust   13

Mantle

Core

Crust

47

47
An odd age to die
In the Prime of life
Not quite the silver age of transition
But the age my momma died

I've been secretly competing with her all of my life.
The urge to succeed her didn't subside
Not even when she closed her eyes

To go beyond college attendance
To not have a baby by 20
To not be plain and simple
To not get Leukemia…

To have others read what I write
To surpass 47 and not die

I am here.
Unearthing.
Realizing.

Understanding that her lane was not mine.

Load

Carried boulders in the suitcase of my mind
The load got so heavy, I tilted a few times

Don't know why I chose to carry all that weight
Or why I allowed other folk's stuff freespace

My own precious cargo couldn't fit inside
I carried everybody's contents with ponderous pride

Didn't even see how unfruitful I was becoming
'Cause everyone complimented me on my carrying
Said I was strong and did a great job of handling

But the seams started ripping as I tipped the scales
And I paid for the weight in tears and cares

Then one day I got tired of paying all those fines
I unpacked, cleared out, and when asked declined

All those Yes(es) that should have been No(s)
I handed them their baggage for them to tote

I'm traveling much lighter and with less freight these days
With just enough capacity to enjoy my stay

Bold Haiku

I'm original
People stop and stare at me
Wherever I go

Picturesque

My Life
Ain't always been picturesque
Been quite pixelated
Sometimes an illusion
With contrasting details and varying speeds
Until the shutter…
The curtain
Allowed light
And
Click… Click…
BE
A new image
Likeness
Artwork known as me

Gone

Supreme loss
Gone In Perpetuity
Dripping lamentations 'cause now
Love is dependent
On Memories
Prayers for peace since understanding
Is more like disbelief

Picking up pieces
Shattered What Have Beens
Fragmented Annual Days
Editing you in
Living...
'Cause you'd want me to win

Worry

Worry?

No way

No ma'am

Not today

Won't be dismayed by trouble in my way

Ain't got time to cry today

Bad thoughts better get away

Ain't s'posed to take thoughts 'bout life anyway.

Lacrimations

When my siblings and I were little, my daddy wouldn't let us cry. If I looked like I was about to drop a tear, he would say, "Yeen' weak," and would tell me to suck it up. Way back then, my daddy believed that tears were signs of weakness. Perhaps it was his military training that caused him to adopt this erroneous and cockamamie belief that he would later in life denounce. It would be years before I, too, learned not to subscribe to holding in tears.

Life definitely brings about change. I now embrace tears and welcome the relief of the release.
I liken tears to a cleansing, especially that of a window or windshield. Spot cleaning and thorough cleansing are necessary for optimal view. Sometimes the climate changes of life bring about floods of tears. These torrential rains sneak up on us and temporarily hamper our sight. When this happens, it's imperative that we pull over, sit, and wait for the downpour to pass.

Doing so allows us to safely navigate through life.

Coin Toss

Gone Away
The Loss is Great
Unfathomable Deprivation
Physical Separation
Painful Feelings of Hammered Defeat

Flip, Toss,
Wail and Rinse
Open. With Your Eyes Now See
A Different Look with Indelible Inscriptions

The Cost is Free
Precious Redemption
Majestic Recovery
Welcoming in Glory
And Hope that One Day a Reunion Will Be

Counted and Collected
Sweet Peaceful Release
Miraculous Comfort
Despite Grief

Escape

Didn't know that mourning you would be so hard
Your instant escape caught me off guard
You said you'd live forever and that we'd never part
I believed you...just didn't know you meant– in my heart

Tell me what were you running from
Who was after you
Did you think I wouldn't have helped you
If you did, that's not the truth

I wish I would've known that you were confined by fear
Maybe I was just too busy; life had clogged my ears
I am working on being available to all you left behind
If one thing your leaving has taught me, I better respect time.

Balance

Too much of this and too little of that
A sprinkle or a shower, just don't hold back
Hold Steady
Gotta make sure things are even
Justice gotta be fair especially in this season
'Cause what's left over ain't always equal

Feelings

Feelings.
We all have them.
Some of us want to appear strong, so we ignore them.
Some of us want to keep peace, so we stow them.
Some of us want to be spiritually grand, so we denounce them.

Feelings.
For those of us who want to heal,
We should acknowledge them.
For those of us who want to be free,
We should name them.
For those of us who want to be delivered,
We should respect them.

We don't have to be led by our feelings, but it is an injustice to self and the people who love us when we disregard them.

Feelings

Laughing

Endorphins releasing
Doubled over in cachinnation
Holding my belly
All teeth are showing
Tears and snorting
Face is hurting from
Undignified chuckling
Roaring and Howling
And Shrieking and Guffawing
Knee slapping and cackling
'Cause I'm overjoyed and happy

Hairess

Somebody told me I had bad hair and boy did I believe them
They made me shame 'cause my hair wasn't trained
And said my look wasn't pleasing
Like most little girls with extra tight curls, my hair went
through many seasons
Of pressing, pulling, and chemical smoothing
To have obedient acceptable tresses

Water and grease couldn't tame my hair
Hot combs and marcels were the necessary hardware
There was no love for my kinky, coily curls
It wasn't cool to be African
Nobody was happy to be nappy and for me no grease worked
magic
There were no creams to make my hair behave well
Just wide tooth combs, hard bristle brushes, and sticky brown
gels

My curls got caged at an early age
They were relaxed, flattened, and straightened
I professed and confessed, that my hair wasn't the best
But this girl's daddy wasn't having it
I guess he grew tired of me speaking the lie, that somehow
began to plague me

He said, **"Yeen got no bad hair. Look at your arms."**

My daddy's words saved me

Took me years to embrace my hair, the strands that God gave
me
Now I rock my hair however I like, 'cause whispers and stares
don't faze me.

Grays Welcome Here

Silver Strays
Wiry Spirals
Lingering near both my temples
Sticking and standing on attention
Making their way
No blending in sight
Unapologetically shouting with all their might
Girl, yo' hair 'bout to be white!

Miss Understood

Miss Understood
Did all she could
To help them grasp and understand
She tried her best
To help with interpretation
But her spin
They couldn't comprehend

It seems they enjoyed their false perception
And ignored her good intentions
Her compassion went beyond their grasp
So she went where she was cherished

Space to Fit

Have you ever tried to fit into a space that didn't seem to stretch, give or bend to accommodate you?

It's like that pair of designer jeans that you bought haphazardly. You didn't feel like trying them on. Your time was limited. AND... BESIDES... FINALLY, the day had come that you were financially fit to make such a purchase. You could afford them. PURCHASE ACCOMPLISHED. Because you are so stoked about wearing these jeans to the next gathering, you hurry home. You get to your humble palace, pull out your floor length mirror, and you jump, you bend, and you sway side to side wiggling making every effort to pull up your new couture threads. Huh? THEY don't move. YOU don't fit. Puzzlement. Bewilderment. Why? What's wrong? They are your size. Now, taking them back would be embarrassing, so you stow them in your closet– always keeping the denim trophies in view. In your heart of hearts, you know that one day you're going to fit. You TRY them on periodically. Some days you are almost able to fasten them, and your hope is renewed, but then there are days when they don't seem to stretch. With every fitting you are careful, because too much force might damage the brand, and technically this pair of trousers has no give. You never give up, but you wonder if you should take a break. You realize your fault in the purchase, and you conclude that at this time there's just not enough space for you to fit.

Some Children

Some children
Learn sooner than others
Some children
Learn what others never will
Some children
Are subjected to illogical lessons, and others are told- just learn
to deal
Some children wake up and go to sleep anxiety filled
While others are comforted and are able to chill
Some children go to school where everthang's supposed to be
cool- constantly being subjected to
Grown folks and their covert teaching coupled with overt
speaking of lies...
Fighting for awards, medals, mere ounces of affection, never
ever receiving honorable mentions
Enlightened? Advanced Classes– you say?
These rulers?
Not even a chance to stand
Labels, fables, the worst kind of fiction
Looked over, passed by, not the right diction
Society's ills, they want us to believe

Nah, never, return those untruths to the sellers...
Might as well sit back and watch our ascension
Cause we ain't playin the game of ill opinion retention

Some Children...
Are Black and Brown Like me

Me, Me, Me

Singing
Me, me, me, me, me
Raised arm
No elbow bend
Hand and fingers wiggling
Over Here crescendoing
Pick Me!
Spastically Begging
To be seen
And heard
Bout to show 'em what I got
Using my words

Oooh, I'm in
But nothing's happening
I don't fit in
I forced my way
Hoping they'd say
I'm what they need
Harmony
The piece that was missing
But they are not moved
By the wonderful things I do
My confidence strays
And in to the quiet excitement fades

Wake up!
What's wrong witchu' girl?
You don't have to fit in their world
Pick yourself up
Shake it off
Sing your song loud and strong
Solo
EVEN IF you have to do it alone

Gracefully move on
They'll soon realize the major loss
While watching you ascend
Using your example
Charting notes on how you are the trend

Liked, Lauded, and Loved

Before my mother's womb, He knew me
Been graced with wonderful family
Given friends who'd lay down their lives for me
Yet, still I struggled with likes and applause and wondered
where was the love for me.

Growing up affirmed daily
By parents who thought the world of me
Accomplished dreams and goals I set for me
Reached many of kids who credit me
Yet, I still waited for likes and applause and wondered where
was the love for me.

Got sisters on top of sisters who celebrate me
And brothers who'd slay giants for looking at me
Received recognition from major entities
Got bookshelves and mantles that hold earned degrees
Everywhere I go folks say they're proud of me
Yet, still I longed for likes and applause and wondered where
was the love for me.

One day I decided it was necessary
To take thoughtful and careful inventory
My findings didn't surprise me
Chile, I was made fearfully and wonderfully
Had forgotten the thoughts He thought towards me
Gathered myself and proclaimed boldly
No need for THEM to validate me
I am loved already.

That Girl

I've had to be IT for quite some time
But now it's my turn
To Receive
To Believe
To Shine

I will no longer be Ms. Come Through
'Cause now I am focusing on what's mine
My dreams
My wants
My cares

I am no longer the IT girl
The Impress Empress
The Heart Loaner
The Anytime Teller

I am now she, her, hers
Who is
Comfortable
In her own skin
Not trying
To blend
The one who
Is unapologetically
Owning
Her fly

That Girl

S'posed to Be

I ain't s'posed to work no 9 to 5
I'm s'posed to be cracking jokes
And making people laugh
I'm s'posed to be travelin' the world eating exotic foods
And sprinkling joy dust on moody moods
I'm s'posed to be front in center on the big stage
Dramatically delivering soliloquies in Broadway plays
I'm s'posed to be encouraging people to live their best lives
And blessing folk with my pretty smile
I'm s'posed to be writing books and penning songs
And humming show tunes all day long
I'm s'posed to be doing what I'm s'posed to be doing.
What in the world am I doing wrong?
Somebody help me 'cause this job ain't no fun.

Truth 'Bout Me

I'm witty and obviously pretty
I hear good music and get giddy
I'm a smart girl with lots of heart
I dibble and dabble in fine arts
I'm a whole mood–I ain't got nothing to prove
I'm silly–I own my quirky
I'm proper...have you seen me chew gum?
I'm loud, but my whisper is a shout
I'm loyal– what did you tell me not to tell her?
I'm unforgettable...you remember my blue hair
I'm free– ain't a box big enough to cage me
I'm a thinker–Sure you ready for my questioning?
I'm Nunu
The only person I gotta be.

In to Me

I love how you are in to me
My hopes
My dreams
My legacy

I love how you crave my inner thoughts
My reasoning
My intellect
My whole being

Because you are in to me
I forever want to breathe the air you breathe
Wake up and you be the first thing I see
Sing your song and be the book you closely read
'Cause you are the only one I want and need

You

You are peace
Assurance
Serenity
Safety

With you I am
At ease
Without inhibitions
Confident
An unlocked door

With you I am
Satisfied
Redeemed
Whole
Restored

Because of You I know love

Reminiscent Recollections

The day will come when memories will be all you have.
Reminiscent recollections of the best laughs
Of the day you wore that special dress
Of the day her words made you want to be your best
Of day his look made you feel extra pretty
Of the day you declared your love publicly
Of the day you first heard that special song
Of the day you slept in his arms all day long
Of the day you realized this girl was home
Of the day you knew he was the one
Of the day you knew she was the rising and setting sun

Cherish every moment before each day is done,
And the regrets you have will be none.

Because.

The day will come when all you have is a memory
Of how amazing life with him, with her used to be.

Sweet Love

Laughing
Smiling
Little Girl Blushing
Singing
Daydreaming
Infatuated Crushing
From your wooing and pursuing
My excitement's accruing
Can't believe I'm preparing
For a night of doing and oooh undoing
For a night of love dripping and extra slow sipping
For a night of thunderous love confessing
For a night of caressing and missing piece connecting
For a night of Dear God, thank you for this blessing

With you.

Learned

I am teachable

Because you have taught me
     That I am worthy
     Of sweet nothings
Of precious thoughts
Of amazing love

Because of you I understand
That I'm special
Unique
One of a kind
Adored

Because of you I know
That I am wanted
Chosen
Desired
Enough

Thank you.

Because of you I've learned

The Kind

I am worthy of love
The kind that gives butterflies
The kind that makes you feel giddy and shy
The kind that makes you close your eyes,
Breathe in slow, and exhale long sighs
The kind that drenches and soaks
The kind that knows
Every inch
Every crevice
Every curve
Every side
The kind that waits
The kind that stays
The kind that satisfies

The kind only you provide

Salt and Light

You're the salt:
Distinctive flavor
Needed in this world
A preserving agent

You're the light:
A beacon of favor
Illuminating hope
Lit representation

Smiling

Gazing at the stars
Dinner in the dark
Feasting on you
Bouncing our intellect
While the cares of this world
The moonlight deflects
Can't keep from smiling
'Cause I know what's next

Mantle

Girl, BYE!

Hunni, Baybeh, Suga, Chile
Who died and made you the standard?
I don't want to be like you (said with a slight neck roll and
emphasis on every last syllable).

The Good Lawd made me who I am and trying to dub you
would be robbing Him of His Gloraay.
Girl puhlease... refined? (sucks teeth) Naw...

I'm raw, pure, and good fuh yah. Get somewhere! Haven't you
heard?
ORGANIC is in now!

Uhmmm huh... Shoot! I'ma respect your stance, but I'ma need
you to respect my gait (squared shoulders, head held high, and
nose tilted at a 45 degree angle).

Girl, BYE!

They

Guess who called me yesterday-
Wanting to talk about what they say

Chile, I almost hung up in her face-
Had to get off the phone and pray

'Cause I'm so tired of they

Who are they anyway

And why they always got something to say

Like somebody died and told them to rule--
Always watching my every move
And offering 2 cents 'bout what I do

Ain't never walked a day in my shoes

They don't know what my life's about

What they say don't even count

They get on my everlasting nerves

They better gon' on somewhere
With their dumb opinions, like I care

-Whatsaname...
Need to stop calling my phone

'Cause I'm good and grown
Always talking 'bout what they say

Body

Is it your own insecurities or perhaps your own desires?
What problem do you have with girls who are genetically
endowed?
How dare you draw attention to her bumps and curves?
EVERY doggone time you see her?

"Ooh you got some big legs."
"Everybody can't wear that dress."
So awfully condescending
But I digress.

Is the turning up of your nose an involuntary motion?
Or did you upon seeing her make that decision?
Should she apologize for her composition?
Or be constantly greeted with your derision?

Why do you ask her if 'dem boys pursue her?
Do you ask that question of every little girl?
Is that how they do it in your world?
What's it to you ma'am or sir?

She's so much more than her physique.
She's a brilliant mind and quite multifaceted.
She doesn't need your unwarranted comments.

Make 'em Pay

Don't Settle
    For Crumbs
        When You're Owed
            The Meal.
                Make 'em pay.

Assumptions

Assumptions killed the relationship–
The business and what could have been.

They robbed you of friendships
Because of wrong interpretations.

They sold you their truth without any proof–
You jumped to conclusions and now you're duped.

Gimme

Gimme my clout
Gimme my credit

I worked too hard for this sh*t
For somebody else to get it

You can ride the wave–
But the recognition is mine
I'm letting everybody know
Who's the originator this time

Gimme my clout
Gimme my credit

I worked too hard for this sh*t
For you to steal it

Green Things

Money
Life
Spring
And
Me

Ain't a darn thang wrong with being green
Don't waste your time hatin' on me
All that jealousy gone stunt yo' esteem

No Harm

Hey girl
I'on mean no harm
Is a preface, a pseudo charm
–An ear piercing alarm
A warning
That harm is about to be done

So when those judgy gift-wrapped words come
Grab your self-respect and run!

Tresses

How sad
That they thought and we thought
And felt the need to
Alter His handiwork to make us more
Palatable
So sad
That we're waiting on laws to be introduced
For it to be okay, acceptable, professional
For us to wear OUR hair
As it grows
From OUR scalps
As if it…We are…
Eyesores

Their Space

I hate this school
It's my momma's choosin'
She thinks it's best for me

All the penny loafer shoes
And crisp collar shirts
Ain't gon' make these folk like me

All these assumptions
'Cause they think I'ma dummy
They just don't know they losin'

I'm tired of stressin'
'bout these microaggressions
They oughta' be tired of pushin'

I don't even respond
To their constant alarms
Careful not to get a violation

I just hope and pray
That my mom will wake
And say, "Boy, their behavior's problematic."

Until that day
I'll navigate their space
Vying for ⅗ o' slice
Then come home alone
Like I do most nights
And allow my tears to quiet me.

I Know Why He's Angry

I know why he's angry
'Cause he's automatically guilty, and it's a sin for him to defend
I know why he's angry
'Cause He can't be a kid like the rest of his friends
I know why he's angry
'Cause you require him to be mute, like good brown boys
s'posed to do
I know why he's angry
'Cause if something comes up missing, your eyes say, I know
you did it
I know why he's angry
'Cause if he aces a test, you assume he must've cheated
I know why he's angry
'Cause if he speaks too loud, you call him hostile
I know why he's angry
'Cause in his skin, he can't be happy
I know why he's angry

It's 'cause your implicity– 'cause you see him as subhuman.

Repeating

Tired of hurting
'Cause you repeating
Ingrained pain
Deep rooted and seated
You forgot how you felt
When you were dealt this treatment?
I'm running out of breath
'Cause my heart you keep beating

Noise

Quit talking all that nonsense
That racket
That loud talk
That smack
Ain't nobody listening to that shhhhh
It's empty
Sounds like cymbals
Clanging and Banging
Like a subway station
With a bunch of off key sangin'

Piggybacking

You ain't got nothing new to say
Is my way the only way
Will your two cents ever make a dime
Or is being original a crime.

Lying Liar

Got me second guessing what I know for sure
Got me around here questioning cause your heart ain't pure
Over there spreading trash you know ain't true
All cause you want folks to uphold you

Tiptoe

My ankles are sore
The balls of my feet are calloused
I've tiptoed so much
I've forgotten how to balance
My shoulders slump over
My head hangs low
All 'cause I gotta tiptoe 'round yo' ego

All this
Dartin' and avoidin'
Feelin' exploited
Carefully dealin'
Witcho' sensitive feelins'
Got me rethinikin' and clearin'
And monitorin' my breathin'

Seeing now more clearly
Done with all this shrinkin'
Standin tall and resilient
I, too, am important
Gotta' new stance and pivotin'

Better watch out I'm comin'
Flat foot stompin'
on eggshells– I'm crushin'
And doing it confidently

Us and Nem

It's a big difference between US and Nem
Our honesty, uprightness, and decency will pay off
No need to focus on their unmitigated gall
Or hope that one day their shenanigans will stall
Right always wins and that's a fact
We don't have to engage in slick talk or theatrical acts
We're okay doing what we do
Long as we mind our business and stick to the truth
Ain't no time for highlighting their crimes
They'll reap what they've been sowing and we'll be just fine

If

If you have the POWER–
The truth
To end a false narrative,
But you don't,
You have an integrity problem

Don't allow untruths to perpetuate
Even if the unveiling,
The uncovering
Reveals you

Core

Witnesses

Precious
Up Yonder
Cloud of Witnesses

Wanda
Sweet... Chill... Wise.
My momma

Authur
Resourceful... Leader... Provider.
Grandaddy

Catherine
Soft... Pure... Gracious.
Gramma

Mae
Fancy... Creative... A whole lotta know-how.
Grandma

Sherman
Advocate... Sage... Protector.
My daddy

Pillars
Gone
My Elders

Catherine's Crew

Kay Kay and Maxine
Mary Louise and Glory Jean
Wanda Joyce and Ricky too
God's masterpiece but Catherine's Crew

Mae's Girls

Lillie
Ann
Caronetta
Carlean
Princesses who belonged to Mae Roy The Queen
Noblewomen of great Substance and Truth
And
Skilled at whatever their hands could do

My Daddy's Brothers

There's
Uncle Chico's camera
And Uncle Pop's morning calls
But nothing like Uncle Jimmy's goodheartedness

There's
Uncle Jimmy's cooking
And Uncle Pop's swagger
But nothing compares to Uncle Chico's prowess

There's
Uncle Chico's physique
And Uncle Jimmy's smile
But nothing like Uncle Pop's couture style

There are
Superheroes
And there are marvelous sidekicks

But there's nobody in the world like my daddy's brothers

Mirror

When I was a little girl, I had a love affair with my grandmother's living room mirror, the one to the right of the front door. I would position myself in just the right spot on her Victorian couch so that I could see my WHOLE self in her oblong, slightly ornate gold trimmed mirror.

My positioning was strategic. You'd think I was the welcoming committee, because my face would be the first one you'd see upon entering the front room. Back in those days, children played in the den or if you were a boy outside, but Sherwanda's favorite place was in the parlor in front of my grandmother's antique mirror.

My staring and glaring wasn't about admiring the reflection looking back at me. It was more about what I wished I could see. I would spend hours just sitting there imagining what I'd look like one day or who I'd be. I'd imagine my nose being smaller. I have my daddy's wide nose. I'd imagine my hair being finer. I have my mommy's coily kinks.

Boy, I'd give anything to go back and look in my grandma's mirror. I'd tell "Dirty Red" -that's what my daddy used to call me- a whole heap of stuff. I'd tell her 'all that talking' is going to make room for you. Hushers will come, but don't allow their volume to overpower yours.

I'd say, Nunu Girl, write your stories 'cause someday people are going to read them. And chile, don't be scared to be different; there's only one you. OH AND... Keep living, one day you're gonna be cute.

If November was a Human

If November was a human,
She'd be a grandma.
A soul salve all cushiony and sweet.
She'd smell like cocoa butter, pound cake, and other yummy
treats.
She'd sing with extra wide and heavy vibrato,
And with the perfect cock, her Sunday hat would sit.
She'd wear a thimble, crochet knit, and with her bare hands sew
and stitch.
She'd shuck corn and shell peas, and the best Sunday dinner
she'd fix.
If November was a human, her name would be Catherine or
Mae. If November was my Grandma, I'd hug her and kiss her,
and beg her to stay.

The House on Parkway

I didn't understand the significance of Parkway until I read about the Black Bourgeoisie in Memphis. Turns out this tree lined avenue was a special street, AND if you were Black and had a residence on the road, you'd achieved a societal victory.

It was my Aunt Gloria Jean's house, but the ownership and pride belonged to us all...the entire Carter-Herron clan. Only certain families lived on Parkway, and for a short time we were one of them. It was the place where we would fellowship, celebrate, and gather.

Life on Parkway was a little different from other streets in South Memphis. Most lawns on Parkway were manicured, and ours was too. We could not play in the front yard, because children frolicking in plain sight was a no-no on our beloved Parkway. Playing was reserved for the backyard.

The outside of the house was one thing, but on the inside, we were our regular Carter/Herron selves-- jovial, jolly, and jubilant. I don't ever remember sadness reigning in that house. I do remember a lot of cackling, partying, and dancing. If you told me there was some struggle, I'd argue with you. We were a celebratory clan who gathered every Lord's Day to observe "Thanksgiving". Our Sunday dinners were festive feasts. We were thankful no matter the season, and the gathering was about more than just food. The togetherness was the highlight.

Every household represented contributed to the meal. I'm sure our menus varied, but I can't help but chuckle thinking about my momma's fascination with Watergate Salad. It was her dessert of choice for a while. It was a cloudy mound of cottage cheese, pecans, jello, fruit cocktail, and imitation whip cream. I don't think many folk ate it, but I did 'cause my momma made it. Sure wish I could REWIND and eat a heaping spoonful of that sweet fluff or even get a whiff of the time back when family was enough.

Wanda's Face

Forehead smooth and wrinkle free
Brows centered symmetrically
Cheekbones chiseled high and emphasized
Symbols of beauty that held up Wanda's eyes
The wisest lookers one would ever see
Cute little nose that pointed perfectly
Smooth skin with invisible pores
Enhancements not needed, only rouge worn
Lips and mouth laughed out loud
And spoke words of wisdom that were profound

My momma's face–

In my dreams thrice she visited me
I could see her features vividly
Her countenance showed she was proud of me.

Grandma Catherine

My grandmother Catherine Herron Carter was the epitome of grace and beauty. I never had unfulfilled expectations when it came to her. She loved me in word AND deed. I was her Nunu, her Nookie. She was the COMPLETE and ABSOLUTE EXAMPLE of come through. She was a waymaker, and her consideration was second to none. Her benevolence was indescribable. I remember feeling extra special the time I got to use her powder blue leather luggage. I thought I was somebody. Grandma was a true servant and seemed to always be in preparation mode. No one in her presence was ever going to go without.

The memories of my girlfriend (my nickname for her) are great. I remember her making crib sheets for the birth of my little cousins. I remember those amazing strawberry cakes, those birthday cards with a couple of dollars, and those photo albums under the coffee table. I remember her arms being selflessly wide open to many. She was an extreme giver of her time and love. Her words were ALWAYS sweet. She didn't get mad often, but when she did, you still felt loved.

I'll Be There

Every concert
Every game
Every play
Nothing will ever keep me away
I'll be there no matter the stage
I'll always have time and attention to pay

I'll buy a ticket no matter the cost
I'll travel miles and many bridges cross
I'll always be your greatest fan
You ain't gone never NOT see me in the stands

And if my yells draw side eyes and stares
I'll cheer even louder saying, "Dat's my baby over there."
So when the words of critics draw fear
I'll be there to affirm and wipe your tears

'Cause I'm your momma
And I'll ALWAYS be there.

Magnificent Melrose Street

Nothing can compare to the fun we had growing up on Melrose Street. There was always a celebration of community and family going on. Our street was full of families. There were the Davises, the Websters, the Ingrams, the Wades, the Yanceys, the Easleys, The Stanleys, The Registers, The Williamses, The Ambroses, and us, The Carters. We had a FAMILY house on both ends of Melrose Street with my grandma Catherine's house being on the north end and my aunt Gloria Jean's house being on the south end. We never had to go far to celebrate or to visit because we were always together on Magnificent Melrose Street.

Fun was our everyday norm, and boredom rarely neared. That's partially because my cousins were always around. We spent most of our time together outside because playing was not allowed in the house. Inside was reserved for eating and sleeping, but outdoors was for memory making, and boy did we make memories. Like the time when I made my cousins Toya and Renee sing songs I'd made up on grandma's porch. Chile, those girls did whatever I told them to do. They would buy a dream from me if I had sold it to them. I guess that was the power of being a big cousin. Big cousins were the definite leaders on Melrose Street with lots of power like my cousin Tesa. She didn't take no mess, and I was a bit puffed up because I knew no one was going to touch Tesa's little cousin. Tesa was also a self-proclaimed choreographer back on Melrose Street. She had an arsenal of majorette routines. She'd have my cousin Courtney, our friend Tressa, and me marching up and down the street while she gave dance commands like, "Tesa's majorettes, are you ready?" We'd shout, YES! One time, we actually had our own parade up and down Melrose Street. Honey, we had on white outfits, and my cousin Robert kept a steady drum cadence on the top of a tin garbage can. Tesa would blow a whistle, and we'd strike a pose.

The summertime was the best time living on Melrose. Competition ruled the street during the summer months. You'd think it was the Olympics with all the gaming going on. Our gaming was greater than any matchup on an electronic device or video game. It was in person with our cousins and our Melrose Street friends. We played games like volleyball, kickball, and relay races. These games brought everybody out including the adults. Our elders would sit on their porches, chat, and watch us compete in the street. Whichever team won owned the rights to talk smack for the rest of the night. And if we were playing dodgeball or O-U-T- Out!, some of the grownups joined in the fun. It always made me laugh to see the grownups run. They seemed to always flail their arms like wet spaghetti. Sometimes we'd play Hide and Go Seek and Red Light, Green Light. And when the temperature rose above 90 degrees, we'd enjoy the blessing of running through the yard sprinklers.

Summertime was the best time. Our days were full and fun on Melrose Street.

Sweet Fay

Hey Girl
Pretty Girl
Dancing Girl
Sassy Girl
Smart Girl
My Daddy's Little Girl

Last night I dreamt of you
Hoping you didn't think I failed you
Hoping you know how much I miss you
Hoping you know just how much I love you

Hey Girl
Pretty Girl
Dancing Girl
Sassy Girl
Smart Girl
My Daddy's Little Girl

I wonder if you know how special you are
How amazingly brilliant you are
How incredibly funny you are
How wanted you are

Hey Girl
Pretty Girl
Dancing Girl
Sassy Girl
Smart Girl
My Daddy's Little Girl

I wish I could hug you real good
Until then I'll watch videos and look at pictures of when times
were good

The day will come though when I'll see you and it'll be for
good
Until then, Sweetpea, I will hold you in my heart and wish you
good

Hey Girl
Pretty Girl
Dancing Girl
Sassy Girl
Smart Girl
My Daddy's Little Girl

I pray You Are Good

From Aye Mane to Amen:
Big Sherman's Eulogy

Long before I saw Toya's face and my Big Brother's eyes and before my FIRST scream, I knew that I was going to eulogize my daddy.

Eulogize- to speak well of

Aye Mane! My daddy, Sherman L. Jones was Memphis. South Memphis, but just as much North Memphis. He was Klondike, Manassas, and Lemoyne Owen. He was North Frayser and Douglas. He was Gaston, He was Sexton, He was O'Brien Park, He was Pine Hill.

Most of us saw Sherman as super human. His cape and suit of armor weren't fancy. His strength– superpower– was service. He was beyond the sphere of a box. He did things his own way. He was a Marvel. He was fearless; nothing really scared him. He was a force to be reckoned with. And honestly, if My daddy saw us crying, he'd Say, "Aye Mane... You wrong!!!" He had a huge roar. If you were afraid of his roar, you really didn't know him because Big Sherman was really gentle in his giantness.

My daddy was territorial. His favorite pronoun was "My". My Shun, My Nunu, My Sherman, My Million, My Kesha, My Dario, and My Fay Fay. My sisters. My brothers.

My daddy, Big Sherman, was representation. He was an advocate, a stand- in, a father figure. My daddy clothed, and he fed. If you played for my daddy, you never had to wash a uniform, because he did (or whichever one of us he told to do it). Just like his biological children, many of you had breakfast prepared for you on Saturday mornings at Gaston or North Frayser Community Center. What did we eat for breakfast? Wright Bacon... Jimmy Dean sausage.... Don't forget the biscuits.

Some can attest to the fact that when there was no place to lay your head, Sherman opened up our home and gave you a place to stay. Our basement was always full.

My daddy would travel miles to sit and visit with his elders. He was the family representative at EVERY funeral. And if you ever got into trouble, Sherman visited you too. And when you had your day in court, Sherman was there to testify on your behalf or just be an audience member for support. He went to graduations. He went to school conferences. Sherman didn't have to conference with school officials often for us, but he did for many in this room.

My daddy was opportunity. He gave a lot of us our first jobs. Y'all remember training? Uniform shirts and blue shorts, box hockey, the lunch truck, Shape-ups, the Beale Street Show, the Mud Derby, Hershey Track and Field?

My daddy was a Beacon of Hope. There is not enough time in the world to sum up what my daddy meant. I could go on for days, but my daddy made me promise not to funeralize him. We are all going to miss our superhero.

No newspaper, comic book, or motion picture could contain HIS story. Sherman's story is a blockbuster, and we are the sequel. So Dee… Nephews, we can be just as great. Dee, you will finish school. Nephews, ain't none of y'all average. Keep your eyes on the prize. 'Cause Shaun, Nunu, Lil Sherman, Cat, Kesha, Dario, Fay Fay- Y'all 'sposed to be better than me. Be patient; it takes time to succeed. Your time gon' come if you take care of your business.

Finally, the saying Amen is what we usually say to seal a prayer. It means "IT is so, So be it, or Truth." [2]

Aye Mane, everything's gone be 'aight.

Aye Mane, AMEN!

2 "Amen." *Lexico.com*. 2022. https://www.lexico.com/en/definition/amen (4 June 2022)

Text Message

Hey Booka Rudis
Glad we got to catch up today. Just wanted to send a little encouragement about them green folk.

They'll point
And
They'll laugh
Let them think they know the half
Don't you stop being you
Keep going
Don't stoop
We don't match energy
We vibrate higher

Don't be a millionaire living under a bridge allowing folk who don't have what you have make you feel bad for having what you have.

Stand still
Keep living
You'll see
Even if they never see

Love Always,
Your #1 Cheerleader
Mom

Mae Roy's Table: Curated Sunday Love

Sunday dinner at my grandparents' home was magical. It was like a feast of manna with Grandma's supply never running out. There was always enough for the crowd that gathered around the big table in the dining room. Everybody was welcome. It didn't matter if you were family or neighbors, your name went into Palermo's Pot.

Grandma's stove and oven were in overdrive every weekend. She began preparing our feast well before the sun set every Saturday night. She would provide a smorgasbord to satisfy everyone's palate. There would be pork, beef, poultry, and vegetables, many straight from Grandaddy's garden. We'd have turnip greens, black eyed peas, fresh corn, lima beans, pasta, yummy wax bean salad, and so much more. No vegetable or side dish was jealous, because they all had their own spot on Grandma's clothed table. And then there was Grandma's special bread, SWEET BUTTERY YEAST ROLLS. For me these flakey clouds of love were the star of the show. They seemed to take the longest to make, but they were worth the wait. I'm not sure what all went into Grandma's rolls, but I can still see that huge green bowl filled with her special dough resting on top of the Frigidaire under a towel. My eyes would stare for what seemed like days in anticipation. Rise. Rolls. Rise!

Grandma was quite the patissier. It was common for us to have cakes, pies, and orange peels intricately cut and stuffed with sweet potato pone topped with melted marshmallows. Her desserts were well sought after. She used no boxes. Everything was homemade. She sifted her own flour, made her own chocolate, and whipped her own frosting spreads.

My grandma, Mae Roy Jones was no cook; she was culinary artistry at its FINEST. OH and her presentation was above sophistication. Every weekend we were in for some fine dining. The table was always beautifully set. I have to admit, I used to have a little anxiety moments before dinner time if I knew we were heading to my grandparents' home. I knew if we landed on Palermo before time to dine, I'd have to help set the table. The sight of my Grandma's silver sent me into panic mode and thinking of places to hide in that big ole house. I still struggle with placement after all these years.

Early arrival came with benefits too. The greatest benefit was being Grandma's taste-tester. I felt extra special knowing that Grandma had my approval before the table was ever spread.

Grandma would be sweating by the time it was time for us all to eat. The beads of sweat running down her face were proof that tons of love went into curating our Sunday dinner. Arthur Lee! Sherman Lee! Charles Albert! Jimmy! She'd call family members by name to let them know to come from the den to the dinning room for grace. Everybody came running because we knew the joy that was about to grace our tongues and fill our stomachs. We'd all join hands, my daddy would crack a joke, she'd give him the eye, and Grandaddy would say the blessing. And all were fed. Grandma would be the last one to eat, but that didn't bother her because she'd rear back with her arms folded and smile and ask us individually, "Did you get enough?"

Power Outage

Early Morn'
Oven On
Counter covered in flour dust
Dough rolled
Biscuits cut
Spaced and laid
Buttered and brushed
In they go to rise I trust
Can't wait to taste that golden brown crust
Strawberry jam... Issa' must
This 'bout to be a good breakfuss-

Flicker... Flicka...

I can hear Florida Evans cuss

Voicemail

Hey Man-Man
It's your Momma callin'
Thought about you today and how you used to be ballin'
I used to love seeing you on that soccer field
Shooting goals, strikin' balls, and executin' bicycle kicks

Boy, you used to be ballin'
You used to be hurtin' 'nem on that basketball court too!
Shakin' em, crossin' em, and breakin' legs

'Member how I used to embarrass you in the stands?
I used to be hollin' and screamin' and you'd gimme that eye
I wudn't shame
I wanted everybody to know you belonged to me
DJ's Momma
Proud

My boy!
Momma used to love seeing you play that piano too!
Ticklin' those keys, bobbin yo' head, rockin' side to side while playin' by ear
You know I had to throw that in 'cause my baby got skills

Well Noodles… you hated when I used to call you that, I'm 'bout to get off this phone. Just wanted to holler atcha. I ain't want nothin'. Call me back.
Sweet Dreams. See ya lata. I love ya.

Cathy the Great

My little sister Cathy is the Greatest.
Her story is vast and must be well documented.
The plot is just so HUGE.
So, as her personal anthologist, I am working to condense a
compilation that would capture a synopsis of our Cathy Boo.

Y'all, I am glad to say there's no ending in view.
THIS book will forever be added to.

I think I'm going to title the collection TRUE.

Check out a few of the chapters her book will include.
She Knows
Honored Sister and her Sister of Honor
November, Twelve Times Two
The Thrivalist
Chillations and Cathyisms
Pure, But Not Afraid of the Dirt
Run, Ran, and Won the Race
Current readers are offering rave reviews!

Spicy Hot Fries... I on't Eat 'Em

The day was overcast, but that ain't never stopped us. We were just happy to be together. First cousins. Sisters' girls. Me and Courtney. Nunu and Bo. On most days you could find us dancing, singing, or playing Punchinella on Melrose Street but not this day. This day was a bike riding day, just me and her riding our bikes down Dunnavant Street, off and on the sidewalk. Jumping curbs. Walking our bikes, front wheels off the ground, still pedaling. Fancy. Us Girls. Riding with no hands on the bars, instead on our hips. It must've been something about hips and hands, 'cause I remembered that I had some change, and change meant hot fries. Me and Courtney were lovers of all things hot: hot sauce, hot tamales, and hot souse. We stopped by the candy lady to get some penny candy and hot fries. Those things were so good, and I probably enjoyed licking my fingers more than chomping on the crunchy sticks. We didn't carry purses, so we put our stuff in our shirt and rode back towards the 'partments. We took a pause-- KICKSTAND Down-- to pop open our bags. In a hurry, I decided to use my teeth instead of pinching and pulling to open my chip bag. The plastic. That plastic. I couldn't breathe. The plastic. "What's wrong witchu, girl?" I tried to say, plastic, but that plastic was covering the whole of my throat, and I couldn't get air. I don't know what happened, but Courtney worked some magic, and that plastic moved away from the hole in my throat. She saved me.

Spicy Hot Fries... I on't eat 'em.

In Memory of Courtney Denise Stanley Hayes
June 17, 1974 - April 4, 2004

Gifted Hands
Iconic Style
And the Most Angelic Smile

Wanda... An Epistle Read by Many

Written text is good, but the experience is better when the text breathes.

If you were blessed to read my momma's story, you know that the underlying theme was peace. She pursued peace and literally embodied serenity. My momma, Wanda Joyce, was always mindful of her space. Her quiet, harmonious character spoke volumes. She was a calming, and you could find safety in her borrowed words. My momma was composed of grace and offered comfort and love to so many. She was a retreat, so much so that even at the end, although quite paradoxical, those who loved her, the avid readers, still had peace.

Wonders

Wonders
I've felt your strength
The warmth of your arms
Heard your voices when I needed calm

Such endearing bonds
Your listening ears didn't come with a price
Felt no judgment when I needed advice
Have you to thank for many of the joys in my life

Thank you for championing me
For positioning yourselves to help me win
You've been an integral part of my growing
And you did it all without smothering

Sweet Wonders
Never taking advantage of my vulnerability
Grateful for the countless things you've done
All while weathering your own storms
You are Wanda's Wonders
An amazing bevy of women
Blessings straight from heaven

College Drop-off

Girl, you have everything you need to thrive.
You've been taught.
GO AND OPERATE in wisdom.

Trinity, you've already won. You are a Victor!
ALWAYS know there's a way that seems right, but there's also a way of escape.
Sis, don't focus too much on weapons.
They form, but you and I both know they AIN'T Gotta or Gonna prosper.
Remember our fights aren't physical.

Use. Your. Words!
AND... Learn to appreciate the beauty of REST and RETREAT.

On days when life throws lemons, tomatoes, pies, table scraps, and crumbs at you, "Chop it up" and do what we do, "make a meal."
Stay sharp. Keep your utensils near.

Find the beauty and the good in every day.

You are loved. As long as you LIVE, you will never go a day without knowing love. You got this honey, because ways have been made for you.

WALK.
AT YOUR OWN PACE.
Your own gait.

June

June smells like Aramis and Jean Paul Gaultier cologne.

It's the sun beaming in the morning and the melody of the sparrow's song.

It's SoftSheen-Carson's Magic Shaving Powder on the butter knife in the coffee mug.

It's the aroma of potatoes, bacon, biscuits, and eggs in the morning and lighter fluid soaked charcoal in the evening.

It's the sound of cranking lawn mowers and weed eaters edging the lawn.

It looks like white tube socks meeting the hem of khaki shorts.

It's the sound of bouncin' balls on slabs of concrete and kickin' it in the park.

June is Big Sherman's month.

Literate

My mama was a writer

My daddy was a reader

I'm a mixture of them both

I can do either

Acknowledgments

I'm thankful for those who have walked alongside me during this process. I am grateful for those who have encouraged me and nudged me to collect and bind my words and experiences, especially my Aunt Maxine. It is because of your support I have been able to pen my heart knowing I have willing readers.

I have my parents to thank for my love for literacy. Our home was filled with print, because both of my parents were avid readers. My mother was a Bible scholar who enjoyed reading inspirational books and journaling. My dad read the newspaper everyday and had a collection of books that included works by Carter G. Woodson and Alice Walker. Books of every genre were in our home. I remember when my parents purchased a brand spanking new set of World Book Encyclopedias. The gems were red with gold lettering. I thought we were rich and lucky because we didn't have to go to the library for homework or projects anymore. My parents were just as excited about the encyclopedia purchase, so much that they went out and bought a new entertainment shelf just so we could have a place to display our new trophies.

Writing has always been a way of escape and expression for me. My first journal was a yellow legal notepad that my dad brought home from his office. I used this makeshift journal to write about everyone and everything, from things I was afraid to say to details about my most memorable situations. Journaling became a means of therapy before I knew what therapy was. *Unearthed* is a continuation of the many entries written on that yellow legal notepad I took from my daddy's briefcase.

My first introduction to expressive writing in a school setting was in Ann Poteat's class at Frayser School. Ms. Poteat taught eighth grade Honors English. She had us write everyday in a notebook. She would have us fold each page vertically leaving one side of the paper blank. On the blank side, she would respond to all of her students' writing. It was sort of a discourse log where we would communicate back and forth in writing. This would be the first time I realized I could write something worth reading. Thank you, Ms. Poteat.

I was never truly concerned about the mechanics of writing until I took a course in college that majored on structure and grammar. I still don't major on punctuation as much as I should because I have my sister Catherine L. Solomon who is a true grammarian. Although I am more than 5 years her senior, she is truly the big sister. Thank you Cat for holding my hand during the writing of *Unearthed* and for ALWAYS encouraging me to tell my stories.

Last but not least, I must show gratitude to my family. Family is important and will always come first after MY HEAVENLY FATHER. I am so thankful that I was born into two amazing clans, the Joneses and the Carters. Because of y'all, I have never known a day without love. Thank you for being my grace and a soft place to land. I am blessed to know that I have people who are waiting and always willing to catch or carry me if needed. To the immediates, Arness, Trin, and DJ, thank y'all for being an inspiration and for loving me and all my extraness. Thank you for always giving me something to write about.

ABOUT THE AUTHOR

Sherwanda Nunu Chism, Ed.D. is a wife and the proud mother of two rising stars. She enjoys writing, reading Young Adult fiction, and listening to various genres of music. Dr. Chism has been an educator for over 20 years. As an educator, Dr. Chism has worked with elementary aged students, students who are intellectually gifted, and those who are English Language Learners. She believes in being a voice for underserved and underrepresented populations and giving all students access to learning by providing culturally relevant curriculum.

Dr. Chism is the host of The Gathering: A Place Where Sisters Meet, a podcast that can be found on multiple streaming outlets.

www.ingramcontent.com/pod-product-compliance
Lightning Source LLC
Chambersburg PA
CBHW020705260626
47157CB00008B/3148